AI AND BIOMEDICAL INNOVATION

a Deep Dive

Roberto Sammarchi

Parma & Sammarchi - Imprese e Diritti

Copyright © 2024 Roberto Sammarchi

All rights reserved

Parma & Sammarchi - Imprese e diritti
Casalecchio di Reno (BO), Italy

First edition - December 2024

parmasammarchi.it

Introduction

Two seminars to provide biomedical engineers with a comprehensive understanding of the European Artificial Intelligence Act and its impact on the healthcare industry and services. We will explore the key provisions of the regulation, discuss its implications for medical device development and clinical practice, and examine case studies to illustrate how the AI Act can shape future biomedical innovations.

Seminar I - AI for Biomedical Engineers: Balancing Innovation and Regulation

Exploring the key provisions of the AI Act and their impact on biomedical engineering.

Cesena, Dec. 10th 2024

Seminar II - AI for Biomedical Engineers: A Compliance Guide

Ensuring your AI projects align with the AI Act's requirements.

Cesena, Dec. 17th, 2024

Seminar I - Ai For Biomedical Engineers: Balancing Innovation And Regulation

Exploring the key provisions of the AI Act and their impact on biomedical engineering.

Cesena, Dec. 10th 2024

This introductory seminar examines the core provisions of the Artificial Intelligence Act and their impact on biomedical engineering. Tailored specifically for biomedical engineers, the session provides a detailed overview of the regulatory implications of the AI Act, with a focus on how these provisions influence medical device development and clinical practices. Key discussions will address the potential risks and benefits of implementing advanced AI technologies in the biomedical sector, with an emphasis on balancing innovation with fundamental rights protection. Through case studies, participants will explore strategies for integrating advanced AI solutions in the biomedical field while adhering to the transparency and safety standards mandated by the Act.

Introduction And Goals

Brief introduction to the seminar's goals. Overview of the Artificial Intelligence Act, its purpose, and its relevance to biomedical engineering. Key objectives: understanding regulatory impacts, risk management, and integrating AI in biomedical fields responsibly.

Artificial intelligence is at the forefront of healthcare innovation, driving advances in diagnostics, patient care, and medical devices. However, as these technologies grow more influential, so does the responsibility to ensure they are used safely, ethically, and transparently. This is where the Artificial Intelligence Act comes in. Designed by the European Union, the AI Act sets out rules to govern AI systems in ways that protect public welfare, uphold human rights, and foster innovation.

The purpose of this seminar is to give you a deep understanding of how the AI Act impacts your work as biomedical engineers and to equip you with the tools to align your projects with this landmark regulation. Compliance with the AI Act is more than a legal requirement; it's a way to build trust in AI technology by prioritizing patient safety, privacy, and transparency.

Background On The Artificial Intelligence Act

Let's start with some background on the Act itself. The Artificial Intelligence Act was introduced to create a harmonized framework for AI across Europe, aiming to prevent market fragmentation, foster responsible innovation, and safeguard the rights of EU citizens. Central to the Act is a risk-based approach that categorizes AI systems by their potential impact on health, safety, and fundamental rights.

For biomedical engineers, this means that AI used in medical devices or clinical applications may fall into the high-risk category, especially when it has a direct impact on patient outcomes. As such, understanding and adhering to the AI Act's requirements are essential to responsibly develop, deploy, and maintain AI systems in healthcare.

Objectives Of Today's Seminar

Today, we'll explore three main objectives:

1. First, we'll look at the core provisions of the AI Act that impact your roles and projects. By examining these regulations, you'll gain insight into how they influence various stages of AI development, from design to implementation in medical devices.

2. Second, we'll discuss the unique challenges and opportunities

that come with integrating AI in healthcare while meeting regulatory expectations. Compliance doesn't have to stifle innovation; instead, we'll see how it can create pathways for trustworthy AI that patients and healthcare providers can rely on.

3. Finally, we'll put these principles into practice through an interactive case study. This exercise will give you hands-on experience in applying the Act's guidelines to a hypothetical AI project in the biomedical field, helping you better prepare for real-world applications.

Seminar Structure And What To Expect

Here's how we'll proceed in today's session:

We'll begin by exploring the core provisions of the AI Act, focusing on key aspects like risk classification, transparency requirements, and safety standards. We'll look closely at how these provisions are tailored for high-risk AI systems in biomedical applications.

Next, we'll move to a discussion on the Act's implications for medical device development and clinical practice - two areas where compliance with these standards is particularly important. We'll discuss strategies for balancing regulatory requirements with the flexibility needed for innovation.

Following this, we'll have a practical case study where you'll work through a compliance scenario in groups. This hands-on exercise will let you apply today's insights, testing how well you can align a biomedical AI project with the AI Act's requirements.

Finally, we'll wrap up with best practices for integrating AI responsibly in biomedical engineering and open the floor for questions.

Engagement And Takeaways

We want today's session to be interactive and valuable, so we encourage you to ask questions, share your experiences, and participate actively. Regulatory landscapes can be complex, but our goal here is to simplify these requirements so you leave with a clear understanding of how to navigate the AI Act effectively.

Throughout the seminar, we'll be providing you with practical resources, like checklists and case study materials, that you can refer to beyond this session. These resources are designed to help you integrate compliance practices into your projects, facilitating not just adherence to the AI Act, but a commitment to responsible and impactful innovation in the biomedical field.

Core Provisions Of The Ai Act

Lecture format with slides and visual aids. Detailed analysis of the AI Act's main provisions, focusing on: Risk classification of AI systems. Transparency and accountability requirements. Safety standards and ethical considerations. Emphasis on how these provisions affect the development of AI-based medical devices and applications.

The AI Act introduces a risk-based regulatory framework for AI systems, especially high-risk applications, and establishes requirements around transparency, accountability, and safety. Biomedical engineers working with AI-driven medical devices or clinical applications will often find these systems categorized as high-risk, which brings with it additional responsibilities.

Risk-Based Classification of AI Systems

The cornerstone of the AI Act is its risk-based classification of AI applications. The Act categorizes AI systems into several levels of risk—minimal, limited, high, and unacceptable. The risk level is determined based on how AI is deployed, the potential impact on health and safety, and the likelihood of infringing on fundamental rights.

For biomedical applications, this means:

High-risk AI systems are those that have significant impacts on patient safety or public health. Medical devices, diagnostic tools, and other clinical applications involving patient care are often classified as high-risk.

Minimal and limited-risk AI systems may include AI used in more administrative or supportive roles that don't impact patient outcomes directly.

High-risk AI systems must meet stringent regulatory requirements. This risk-based approach provides flexibility but imposes stricter standards on applications where public safety and health are directly involved.

Mandatory Requirements for High-Risk AI Systems

When a system is deemed high-risk, it must meet a series of mandatory requirements to be legally used in the European market. These requirements aim to ensure that high-risk AI systems are safe, transparent, and trustworthy.

Risk Management System

The AI Act mandates that a comprehensive risk management system be integrated into the lifecycle of all high-risk AI systems. This involves:

Conducting regular risk assessments from design through deployment. Implementing safeguards to address identified risks. Continuously monitoring and adapting the risk management approach as the system is updated or as new information arises. For biomedical engineers, this means embedding a risk-focused culture throughout the AI system's development and continuously updating risk protocols based on new data.

Data Governance

High-risk AI systems must follow stringent data governance protocols, especially around data used for model training. Requirements include:

Ensuring that data used in training, validation, and testing is of high quality, representative, and free from biases that could lead to unfair outcomes.

Protecting data privacy and confidentiality, particularly when personal health information is involved, as this falls under both the AI Act and the General Data Protection Regulation (GDPR).

For instance, an AI model trained to detect diseases must be trained on diverse datasets to ensure it doesn't produce biased or inaccurate results for different demographics.

Technical Documentation and Record-Keeping

High-risk AI applications require detailed technical documentation that tracks the AI system's development, functionality, and intended purpose. Documentation must:

Provide a clear explanation of how the AI model operates, its expected outcomes, and its limitations. Include details about data sources, model architecture, and validation methods.

Be continuously updated and made accessible to authorities upon request. In biomedical engineering, maintaining detailed documentation is essential not only for compliance but also for providing transparency to healthcare professionals and patients who rely on these tools.

Transparency and Information Provision Requirements

Transparency is a core principle of the AI Act, particularly for high-risk AI systems that impact healthcare. Transparency requirements include:

Informing users, such as healthcare providers or patients, when they are interacting with an AI system. This is crucial in medical settings, where knowing that an AI system is assisting in diagnosis or treatment decisions allows for informed consent and understanding.

Providing clear information on the system's capabilities, intended uses, and limitations, so that users have realistic expectations. For example, an AI-driven diagnostic tool should clearly inform users of its decision-making limits—if it's highly accurate in detecting specific diseases but less so with others, that information should be openly shared.

Post-Market Monitoring and Reporting Obligations

The AI Act emphasizes ongoing post-market monitoring to ensure that AI systems remain compliant and effective after deployment. For high-risk AI systems, this involves:

Monitoring the system's performance and safety continuously.

Reporting significant incidents or malfunctions to relevant regulatory authorities.

Documenting updates or modifications to the AI system and assessing their impact on compliance and safety.

For example, if a biomedical AI system used in a hospital starts generating inconsistent results or there's evidence of malfunction, it must be reported and, if necessary, the system pulled from service until adjustments are made.

Conformity Assessment and Interaction with Notified Bodies

High-risk AI systems require a conformity assessment before they can be marketed or deployed. For biomedical AI applications, this often means working with an independent notified body that will:

Evaluate the system to confirm it meets all regulatory requirements.

Issue a certification if the system complies, which is necessary for legal market entry.

Working with notified bodies helps ensure the AI system's safety and provides a credible assurance to both healthcare providers and patients.

Penalties for Non-Compliance

Finally, it's essential to understand that non-compliance with the AI Act can lead to significant penalties.

These can include:

Fines for organizations failing to meet mandatory requirements.

Potential removal of AI systems from the market if they pose a risk to health or safety.

Biomedical engineers must prioritize compliance not only to avoid penalties but to reinforce public trust and uphold the credibility of AI innovations in healthcare.

Conclusion and Transition to next step

In summary, these core provisions of the AI Act set out a comprehensive framework to ensure that AI systems, especially those in high-risk categories like healthcare, are designed and used responsibly.

For biomedical engineers, understanding and integrating these requirements is essential for ethical and safe AI implementation. As we move to the next segment, we'll explore how these provisions directly impact medical device development and clinical practice, looking at the specific challenges and strategies involved in balancing regulatory compliance with technological innovation.

Implications For Medical Device Development And Clinical Practice

Case study presentations with interactive Q&A. Exploration of how the AI Act impacts medical device development and clinical applications. Discussion on balancing compliance with innovation, particularly in a clinical setting.

This part of the seminar will cover how the AI Act shapes the design, deployment, and real-world use of AI-driven medical devices. To keep things interactive, we'll explore two case studies that highlight the balance between regulatory compliance and innovation in clinical settings. Each case study will be followed by a Q&A to discuss specific challenges and insights.

Case Study 1: AI in Diagnostic Devices

Let's start with a case study on AI in diagnostic imaging. Consider a diagnostic AI tool designed to analyze medical scans, such as MRIs or CTs, to detect early signs of disease. Due to its potential impact on patient outcomes, this tool is classified as high-risk under the AI Act, which means it must comply with strict safety, transparency, and data requirements.

Risk Management and Patient Safety: Under the AI Act, risk management begins in the design phase. This diagnostic AI tool must undergo rigorous testing to ensure it doesn't generate inaccurate or biased results. For example, if the tool has been trained predominantly on images from a specific demographic, it could perform inconsistently with other groups. Compliance requires diverse, high-quality datasets to ensure reliable outcomes across varied populations.

Transparency Requirements for Clinical Use: Transparency is critical for high-risk tools in medical contexts. This diagnostic AI tool must provide clear documentation about its functionality, limitations, and potential error rates. Clinicians need accessible, understandable information to effectively interpret and trust the AI's results, supporting informed decision-making in patient care.

Data Governance: The tool must comply with strict data quality standards to ensure ethical and effective performance. All training data must be representative and sourced responsibly, with privacy protections in place to comply with both the AI Act and GDPR standards.

Interactive Q&A for Case Study 1

Reflecting on this case study, how would you address the need for transparency while also ensuring that the tool remains user-friendly for clinicians? Do you see any particular challenges in meeting data diversity requirements? (Pause for participant responses and brief open discussion).

Case Study 2: AI for Patient Monitoring in Clinical Settings

For our next example, let's examine a real-time patient monitoring system powered by AI. This system is used in hospitals to monitor patients' vital signs and alert healthcare providers to critical changes. Classified as high-risk due to its potential impact on patient safety, this system also falls under the strictest requirements of the AI Act.

Balancing Compliance and Responsiveness: Patient monitoring systems aim to improve outcomes through real-time alerts. Under the AI Act, however, the system's design must prioritize safety and reliability without compromising its speed or functionality. Compliance in this case involves a careful balance between adhering to regulatory safety standards and maintaining the device's responsiveness in a dynamic clinical setting.

Post-Market Surveillance and Incident Reporting: Once deployed, ongoing performance monitoring and incident reporting are required by the AI Act. For instance, if the system issues false alarms or misses critical changes, these incidents must be documented and reported for regulatory review. Such feedback can inform updates and refinements, but it also highlights the need for consistent vigilance to address emerging risks in real-time.

Data Privacy and GDPR Compliance: Given that this system processes sensitive health data, it must ensure data privacy and protection measures. Not only does the data need to be securely stored and managed, but the AI Act also requires comprehensive documentation of data sourcing, processing, and handling practices to ensure compliance with both the AI Act and GDPR.

Interactive Q&A for Case Study 2

With this example in mind, how would you manage post-market surveillance to ensure the monitoring system remains compliant while responding to real-time data? What unique challenges might arise in patient monitoring that differ from diagnostic tools? (Open the floor for responses and brief discussion).

Balancing Compliance and Innovation in Clinical Settings

As we've seen in these examples, high-risk AI systems in healthcare must navigate a delicate balance between regulatory compliance and the flexibility required for innovative, responsive performance. Let's discuss a few key takeaways and strategies for managing this balance:

Integrating Compliance into Design: By incorporating compliance from the design phase onward, biomedical engineers can meet regulatory standards without compromising innovation. For example, modular risk assessment at each phase allows teams to adjust AI system functions responsively while staying aligned with safety requirements.

Transparency for Trust: Especially in clinical settings, compliance with transparency requirements builds trust among clinicians and patients. Ensuring accessible documentation and clear guidance on AI limitations supports informed decision-making and fosters trust in AI-driven tools.

Continuous Improvement through Post-Market Monitoring: Regulatory compliance doesn't stop at deployment. Post-market surveillance, required by the AI Act, enables teams to continuously refine and improve AI systems based on real-world feedback, keeping them aligned with clinical needs and safety standards.

Let's conclude with a few final questions.

How can we as engineers and developers support both innovation and compliance in our projects?

Are there specific strategies or approaches for balancing these priorities?

(Pause for participant responses, highlighting key shared insights.)

Conclusion and Transition to next Step

To wrap up, we've explored two real-world applications of AI in healthcare, identified compliance challenges, and discussed how to innovate responsibly within the AI Act's framework. As we transition into our interactive workshop, you'll have the opportunity to apply today's insights directly to a hands-on case study in biomedical AI development.

Interactive Case Study Workshop

Hands-on group work on a hypothetical case. Participants apply seminar knowledge to analyze a biomedical AI project and discuss strategies for compliance with the AI Act. Focus on identifying potential risks and aligning project goals with regulatory requirements.

(Participants received in advance 3 forms containing a list of topics to be addressed and are invited to choose and fill out 1 of them, by indicating the main issues to be discussed; further in-depth exploration will be possible in Seminar II).

This session is designed to help you apply the insights we've discussed so far, particularly around compliance with the AI Act, to a hypothetical but realistic biomedical AI project. Working in small groups, you'll assess a project, identify potential risks, and develop strategies to ensure alignment with regulatory requirements.

Workshop Overview

In this exercise, you'll analyze a hypothetical AI-driven medical device case, addressing the compliance challenges involved. After working in groups, each team will share their findings, and we'll discuss the strategies you've developed.

This workshop focuses on three primary tasks:

Identifying Key Compliance Challenges in developing AI for biomedical applications.

Developing a Risk Management Strategy aligned with the AI Act.

Proposing Documentation and Transparency Measures to support regulatory compliance.

Case Study - AI-Enhanced Diagnostic Tool Case Scenario

Imagine you're part of a development team working on an AI-powered diagnostic tool designed to detect early signs of cardiovascular disease from patient data. This tool uses a machine learning model trained on historical data, including a combination of imaging scans, lab results, and patient medical histories. The tool aims to support healthcare providers by analyzing complex data patterns and identifying early risk factors for cardiovascular issues.

Due to its role in influencing patient outcomes, this diagnostic AI tool is classified as high-risk under the AI Act, meaning it must comply with all relevant regulatory requirements, including risk management, data governance, transparency, and post-market monitoring.

Group Work Instructions

Participants in each group should only fill out the form related to the task assigned to their group.

Each group will focus on one aspect of the case, assessing the tool's compliance needs and developing a strategy to address the specific requirements of the AI Act. In your group discussions, consider the following points and prepare to present your solutions.

Task Group 1: Identify and Address Compliance Challenges

Start by identifying key compliance challenges for this diagnostic AI tool. Based on the AI Act's requirements for high-risk systems, consider the following:

Data Quality and Diversity:

What challenges might arise in ensuring that the training data is representative and free from biases?

How would you address any data quality issues that could impact the accuracy or fairness of the diagnostic tool's assessments?

Risk Management:

What are the potential risks associated with this diagnostic AI tool? Consider risks such as false positives/negatives, data privacy concerns, and the impact of demographic variability on diagnostic accuracy.

How will you assess and mitigate these risks during both development and post-market phases? Documentation:

What technical documentation should be prepared to comply with the AI Act? Think about how you'd document data sources, model design, validation methods, and limitations.

How will you fulfill the requirement of transparency?

Task Group 2: Develop a Risk Management and Monitoring Strategy

Your next task is to create a risk management and monitoring strategy that aligns with the AI Act's requirements for high-risk devices.

Focus on these areas:

Risk Assessment Protocols: Outline a risk assessment protocol to be conducted at each phase of development. Consider how you'd handle issues like potential biases, model accuracy, and any clinical errors the system could introduce.

Post-Market Surveillance: Develop a plan for post-market monitoring to ensure the tool performs as expected in clinical settings.

How would you gather real-world performance data, document incidents, and respond to emerging risks?

What mechanisms could you put in place to adjust the system based on new data or identified issues?

Incident Reporting: Identify how you'd comply with incident

reporting requirements.

If the tool generates unexpected results, like consistently missing signs of disease in certain demographics, how would you document, report, and address this issue?

Task Group 3: Plan for Transparency and User Communication

Transparency is a core requirement for high-risk AI systems in healthcare. Discuss how you'd ensure transparency for clinicians and patients using this diagnostic tool:

User Documentation: Create an outline of the user documentation that would accompany the tool. Consider what healthcare providers need to know about the AI's functionality, limitations, and error rates to use it effectively and responsibly in clinical settings.

Patient Transparency:

How would you communicate to patients that an AI is involved in their diagnosis? Consider ways to explain the role of AI in non-technical terms, addressing patient concerns about privacy, reliability, and accuracy.

Regular Updates: Plan for how you'd provide ongoing updates to users about changes, improvements, or emerging limitations of the diagnostic tool, ensuring transparency throughout its lifecycle.

Group Presentations And Discussion

Once you've completed your group discussions, we'll gather for a series of brief presentations. Each group will have a few minutes to share their findings and proposed solutions.

Group 1 (Compliance Challenges)

Present your approach to identifying and managing compliance challenges for the diagnostic tool, including data quality, risk assessment, and documentation.

Group 2 (Risk Management and Monitoring Strategy)

Share your proposed risk management plan, covering risk assessment, post-market surveillance, and incident reporting strategies.

Group 3 (Transparency and Communication)

Describe your strategies for ensuring transparency with both clinicians and patients, highlighting key aspects of user documentation, patient communication, and regular updates.

Conclusion and Transition to next step

This case study exercise has shown how the AI Act's requirements translate into concrete steps in developing an AI-based diagnostic tool.

Here are some key takeaways:

Data Governance and Diversity: Ensuring diverse, high-quality data is essential to reduce biases and improve accuracy across patient demographics.

Ongoing Risk Management: Compliance doesn't stop at deployment; post-market surveillance and incident reporting are critical to maintaining safety and adapting to real-world conditions.

Clear and Transparent Communication: Effective transparency strategies foster trust, supporting both clinician confidence and patient understanding of AI's role in their healthcare.

As we move forward, remember that these strategies not only help you meet regulatory requirements but also enhance the ethical and practical value of your AI innovations in healthcare.

Best Practices For Integrating Ai In Biomedical Engineering

Lecture format with slides and visual aids. Overview of best practices for AI integration in biomedical engineering, considering safety, transparency, and patient trust. Emphasis on aligning AI innovations with regulatory standards without stifling innovation.

This section will focus on strategies that balance regulatory compliance with innovation, ensuring that AI technologies in healthcare enhance safety, transparency, and patient trust.

Design with Compliance in Mind

To align AI innovations with the AI Act's regulatory standards, it's essential to integrate compliance considerations from the earliest stages of development. Adopting a compliance-by-design approach helps anticipate potential regulatory challenges, streamlining the certification process and ensuring smoother integration into healthcare settings.

Proactive Risk Assessment

Conduct iterative risk assessments at each stage, embedding safety features into the design. By continuously evaluating potential risks, such as model drift or biases, teams can adjust the design early to reduce rework or costly modifications later.

Cross-functional Teams

Engage professionals from regulatory, legal, data science, and clinical fields in the design phase. This collaboration encourages a comprehensive understanding of both regulatory and technical requirements, fostering a multidisciplinary approach to problem-solving.

Prioritize Transparent Design and Functionality

Transparency is not only a requirement under the AI Act but also a best practice for building trust. Providing clear, accessible information on how an AI system works and its limitations supports informed use by clinicians and confidence among patients.

Interpretable AI Models

Develop AI systems with interpretable or explainable models where possible. This allows healthcare providers to understand and validate AI-generated results, making AI-assisted decisions more reliable.

Clear User Documentation

Create user-friendly documentation that explains the model's functionality, data sources, and accuracy levels. This helps healthcare providers use the AI system responsibly and understand the boundaries of its effectiveness, improving its acceptance and utility in clinical practice.

Build a Robust Data Governance Framework

Data quality and governance are crucial for maintaining the integrity, fairness, and accuracy of AI models in biomedical applications. Implementing strong data governance practices ensures that AI systems are effective across diverse populations, while meeting ethical and regulatory standards.

Diverse, High-Quality Data

Use representative datasets that cover a wide demographic range to avoid biases and ensure fair outcomes. This practice not only complies with AI Act requirements but also enhances the reliability and inclusiveness of AI applications in healthcare.

Data Documentation and Audits

Establish a structured approach for documenting data sources, preprocessing steps, and quality checks. Regular audits of data management processes can help identify any compliance gaps, enabling corrective actions before they impact patient outcomes.

Implement Continuous Monitoring and Improvement

Even after deployment, AI systems in healthcare should be actively monitored to ensure ongoing safety, accuracy, and effectiveness. Continuous monitoring allows teams to respond to real-world performance data, adapting the system as necessary to meet clinical demands and regulatory requirements.

Post-Market Surveillance

Set up mechanisms to collect and analyze feedback from healthcare providers and end users, identifying any emerging risks or limitations in real-time use.

Regular Model Updates and Retraining

AI models can degrade over time due to changes in patient populations or medical practices. Schedule periodic updates or retraining sessions to maintain high standards of accuracy and relevance, improving patient outcomes while upholding regulatory compliance.

Foster Ethical Use and Patient Trust

Ethical considerations and patient trust are foundational to AI's success in biomedical engineering. By prioritizing responsible use, transparency, and respect for patient privacy, AI developers can create systems that not only comply with regulations but also gain lasting acceptance in healthcare.

Transparent Patient Communication

Inform patients when an AI system is involved in their diagnosis or treatment, providing accessible explanations of the AI's role. This builds patient trust and supports ethical, transparent interactions.

Privacy-Respecting Design

Integrate privacy protection into AI models by using anonymized or pseudonymized data whenever possible. Such practices meet both GDPR and AI Act standards, emphasizing a commitment to patient privacy.

Conclusion and Transition to next step

Innovation within Ethical Boundaries - In summary, following best practices for integrating AI into biomedical engineering not only ensures regulatory compliance but also strengthens the value and acceptance of AI technologies in healthcare.

By proactively addressing safety, transparency, and patient trust, biomedical engineers can create AI solutions that are both innovative and aligned with ethical standards.

As we conclude, remember that regulatory alignment does not have to limit creativity. Rather, it serves as a framework for responsible innovation, guiding the development of AI applications that enhance patient care while safeguarding public trust.

Let's move forward into our Q&A session to address any questions you may have on these best practices.

Q&A And Discussion

Open floor for participant questions and discussion points. Focus on any unclear aspects of the AI Act, practical compliance strategies, or specific challenges in biomedical engineering.

Summary And Key Takeaways

We'll wrap up with a summary of the main points covered and a few key takeaways that you can apply in your roles as biomedical engineers working with AI.

Core Provisions of the AI Act

We began by examining the fundamental requirements of the AI Act, particularly for high-risk AI systems in healthcare. These include standards for risk management, data governance, transparency, and post-market monitoring—all aimed at ensuring that AI systems are safe, ethical, and trustworthy in clinical applications.

Implications for Medical Device Development and Clinical Practice: Next, we discussed how the AI Act impacts various stages of AI development in biomedical engineering. Through real-world examples, we saw how regulatory compliance can support innovation while protecting patient safety and fostering trust.

Interactive Case Study Workshop: In our hands-on session, you worked through a hypothetical case to apply AI Act principles to a biomedical AI project, focusing on compliance challenges, risk management, and transparency. Your strategies reflected the practical steps needed to align with regulatory standards while maintaining flexibility in design.

Best Practices for Integrating AI: Finally, we outlined best practices for integrating AI into biomedical engineering. This included strategies for designing compliant systems, prioritizing transparency, implementing robust data governance, and building trust with patients. These practices ensure not only regulatory compliance but also the ethical and effective use of AI in healthcare.

Key Takeaways

As you leave today's session, here are some core takeaways to guide your work with AI in biomedical applications:

Compliance as a Continuous Process: Regulatory alignment isn't a one-time task but an ongoing commitment. Integrate compliance from the start and maintain it through regular monitoring, updates, and post-market surveillance to keep systems safe and effective over time.

Transparency Builds Trust: Clearly communicating the role, functionality, and limitations of AI systems—both to clinicians and patients—strengthens trust and enhances responsible AI usage in clinical practice.

Data Quality is Foundational: Using high-quality, diverse data ensures fair and accurate outcomes across varied patient populations. Robust data governance practices not only comply with regulations but also improve the reliability of AI applications in healthcare.

Balance Innovation with Safety: Regulatory standards are there to support safe, ethical AI innovations. Compliance by design doesn't limit creativity but rather guides it within a framework that protects patients and aligns with public expectations for AI in healthcare.

Seminar II - Ai For Biomedical Engineers: A Compliance Guide

Ensuring your AI projects align with the AI Act's requirements.

Cesena, Dec. 17th, 2024

This second seminar focuses on ensuring compliance with the AI Act for artificial intelligence projects in the biomedical sector. The session will outline essential guidelines to ensure that AI solutions meet European regulatory standards, with a focus on documentation requirements, transparency, and risk management.

Participants will learn best practices for achieving compliance, including post-market surveillance and monitoring procedures, which are crucial for the application of AI in medical devices. This seminar offers an opportunity to discuss how to align AI project development with regulatory requirements, optimizing the path from design to market.

Recall of essential concepts

Let's get back to the central question: what is the "material" scope of application of the European Regulation on Artificial Intelligence?

The answer is: information processing systems including inference.

Calculation vs. Inference: Bridging Mechanics and Conceptual Reasoning

"A profound contrast seems to emerge between the mechanics of numerical operations and the intellectual exploration that transforms premises into richer conclusions. Calculation tends to remain anchored to algorithmic procedures, strictly defined rules guiding toward a precise result, such as the product of two numbers or the application of a function to a given input. Inference, on the other hand, suggests a conceptual leap: it does not merely manipulate values but delves into logical relationships to deduce new statements, extracting knowledge not explicitly contained in the initial premises.

It is as if calculation follows a predetermined path, without unforeseen deviations, while inference builds a bridge between what is known and what can logically be discovered. A computer can perform calculations with sheer processing power, but when it comes to inference, it becomes crucial to have logical rules, systems of deduction, theories of meaning, and even semantic context. Calculation: arithmetic, functions, equations. Inference: syllogisms, formal logic, deductions, reasoning, even interpretation of data and evidence.

The difference thus lies in the very nature of the process: calculation applies an algorithm, while inference evaluates the consequences of an informational scenario. In literature, for instance in symbolic logic, inference is the process of deriving coherent assertions from already accepted ones, whereas calculation involves the execution of a set of formal or numerical operations. Both are essential, yet each serves a profoundly distinct purpose and nature." [ChatGPT 4o1, Dec. 14th, 2024]

Scope and application of the EU AI Act

The scope of application of the European Regulation on Artificial Intelligence (AI Act) encompasses all AI systems that utilize techniques such as machine learning, logic-based models, statistical inference, and other approaches for processing data to generate outputs like predictions, recommendations, or decisions that affect physical or digital environments.

It applies to:

AI systems developed or used within the EU, regardless of where they were designed or implemented.

AI systems placed on the EU market, including those provided by non-EU entities targeting the European market.

AI systems with effects in the EU, even if they operate outside the EU but impact European citizens.

Purpose: The AI Act aims to ensure that AI systems are used in ways that are safe, transparent, and accountable, while protecting fundamental rights, security, and the values of the European Union. It seeks to manage risks proportionately, focusing on high-risk applications, while fostering innovation and trust in AI technologies.

Introduction and Goals of Seminar II

Brief overview of seminar objectives, focusing on practical compliance with the AI Act in biomedical projects. Explanation of the relevance of compliance in the context of AI-driven medical devices and clinical applications. Outline of the session, emphasizing practical takeaways and resources.

In this session, we will shift our focus to the practical side of compliance — how to navigate and implement the specific requirements of the AI Act in your biomedical projects. Our aim is to translate regulatory requirements into actionable steps, making compliance an integral part of your workflow as you develop AI-driven medical devices and clinical applications.

The Importance of Compliance in AI-driven Biomedical Innovation

Compliance under the AI Act is about more than simply meeting legal requirements; it's about embedding safety, transparency, and trust into the heart of biomedical innovation. The specific demands of healthcare AI — such as managing sensitive patient data, ensuring consistent safety standards, and addressing the ethical dimensions of healthcare technology —make compliance both a practical necessity and a foundation for responsible innovation.

For biomedical engineers, compliance offers three essential advantages:

Patient Safety and Ethical Responsibility: By aligning your

projects with the AI Act, you're ensuring that your innovations prioritize patient welfare. In high-risk AI systems, where the impact of AI can be profound, compliance serves as a critical checkpoint to minimize risk and ensure reliable outcomes.

Sustainable Innovation in Clinical Practice: Compliance frameworks enable you to innovate sustainably, helping to mitigate risks that could otherwise hinder the long-term success of your projects. By setting a strong compliance foundation, you pave the way for scalable and trusted AI solutions.

Efficient Market Access: Compliance not only meets regulatory obligations but also eases the process of bringing your AI solutions to market across Europe. A structured compliance approach can reduce delays and support seamless certification and approval for your products.

Objectives of Today's Seminar

Today's seminar will provide you with a practical compliance toolkit to navigate the AI Act in your work. Here's what we'll focus on:

Breaking Down Compliance into Practical Steps: We'll guide you through the specific compliance steps required at each stage of AI development, from data governance and risk assessment to real-world monitoring. By translating the Act's requirements into actionable practices, we aim to simplify compliance for high-risk biomedical AI projects.

Addressing Compliance Challenges and Solutions: We'll explore common challenges encountered when integrating compliance in AI for biomedical applications, such as maintaining transparency while protecting intellectual property or balancing clinical innovation with regulatory demands. Real-world strategies will help you overcome these barriers.

Providing Compliance Resources for Immediate Application: Today's session will equip you with checklists, templates, and guides tailored to the compliance needs of AI in healthcare, so that you have a clear path forward after this seminar.

Session Outline

Our time together will be structured to build a comprehensive understanding of compliance as a practical tool, not just a regulatory requirement. Here's how we'll proceed:

Core Compliance Requirements for AI in Biomedical Projects: We'll start with a focused look at the AI Act's primary compliance requirements, including data management, documentation standards, and transparency obligations specific to healthcare.

Step-by-Step Compliance Workflow: Next, we'll break down the workflow for embedding compliance into AI projects. From early-stage planning to post-market adjustments, this section covers the essential elements to ensure your projects align with regulatory standards at each phase.

Case Study and Interactive Discussion: We'll apply today's insights to a practical case study, where you'll work through a hypothetical AI biomedical project, identifying compliance strategies and solutions for real-world application.

Key Takeaways and Resources: To wrap up, we'll provide a summary of the most effective compliance practices discussed and distribute resources, including templates, checklists, and reading materials, to guide your compliance journey beyond today.

Practical Takeaways

Our goal today is to empower you with tools and approaches that make compliance not only manageable but beneficial to your innovation process. By the end of this session, you should be able to:

Implement step-by-step compliance processes for high-risk AI applications in biomedical engineering.

Use a compliance-focused approach that integrates smoothly into AI project workflows, supporting both safety and innovation.

Leverage the resources provided for efficient compliance management, from risk assessment templates to data documentation checklists.

Conclusion and Transition to next step

Let's dive into the core compliance requirements under the AI Act and explore how these principles can guide you in creating safe, compliant, and innovative AI solutions in healthcare.

Overview Of AI Act Compliance Requirements

Lecture with slides and documentation aids. Detailed examination of the core compliance requirements of the AI Act, with a focus on: Documentation standards and transparency. Risk management and assessment for high-risk AI systems. Post-market surveillance and continuous monitoring. Special emphasis on the specific responsibilities for developers and deployers of AI in biomedical settings.

In this segment, we'll dive into the core compliance requirements of the AI Act for high-risk AI systems, particularly in biomedical applications. Our focus will be on three main areas:

Documentation and transparency

Risk management

Post-market surveillance

By the end of this session, you should have a clear understanding of your responsibilities as developers and deployers of AI in healthcare, ensuring your systems meet regulatory standards from development through deployment and beyond.

Documentation Standards and Transparency Requirements

Let's start with documentation and transparency, a cornerstone of the AI Act for high-risk AI systems.

Comprehensive Documentation: High-risk AI systems require

detailed technical documentation, which must be available throughout the lifecycle of the AI project. This documentation includes records of system design, development processes, data sources, testing procedures, and risk assessments. For biomedical applications, this documentation should detail:

Model Architecture and Functionality: Clear explanations of how the AI system operates, including model structure, parameters, and processing logic.

Training Data and Data Processing: A record of data sources, how data was processed, and any steps taken to ensure data quality. This is particularly relevant in healthcare, where bias or errors in training data can lead to adverse clinical outcomes.

Testing and Validation Results: Evidence of the model's accuracy, reliability, and limitations, particularly in medical contexts where patient safety is at stake.

Transparency for End-Users: In clinical settings, transparency is essential to build trust. The AI Act mandates that users, such as healthcare providers, understand the AI's functionality, limitations, and how it arrives at its conclusions.

For developers, this means creating:

User-Focused Documentation: Accessible, non-technical explanations of the AI's purpose, intended use, and limitations. This allows healthcare providers to interpret AI outputs accurately and responsibly.

Clear Communication of Model Boundaries: Transparency also includes being upfront about situations where the AI system may not perform optimally. For instance, an AI diagnostic tool should inform users if its accuracy is lower for certain demographics or conditions.

Responsibilities for Developers and Deployers: As developers, it's your responsibility to create and maintain thorough documentation and transparency resources. For deployers - those implementing the AI system in clinical settings - the emphasis should be on training users to understand and navigate these materials effectively.

Risk Management and Assessment for High-Risk AI Systems

Next, let's discuss risk management and assessment, which is crucial for any high-risk AI application, especially in biomedical engineering.

Risk Management System: The AI Act requires an end-to-end risk management system for all high-risk AI applications. This involves conducting risk assessments at each stage of development and continuously evaluating risks post-deployment.

Here's what this entails in a biomedical context:

Identification and Mitigation of Potential Risks: Begin with identifying potential risks associated with your AI system, such as incorrect diagnoses, biased predictions, or data privacy concerns. For each identified risk, outline specific mitigation strategies.

Iterative Risk Evaluation: Risk management is an ongoing process. Each update or modification to the AI system should prompt a new risk assessment. For example, if you modify an AI diagnostic tool's algorithm to improve accuracy, you must re-evaluate its impact on safety and compliance.

Documentation of Risk Management Actions: Keep detailed records of identified risks, mitigation measures, and any actions taken to address these risks. This documentation is crucial for both internal quality control and regulatory compliance.

Specific Risk Management Strategies in Biomedical Settings:

Bias Prevention and Data Quality: Ensuring data quality and diversity is vital to prevent biased outcomes, particularly in healthcare, where disparities in data representation can directly affect patient outcomes.

Monitoring of Model Performance: Regular performance checks can identify if the AI system's accuracy is changing over time or if it's producing erroneous outputs under certain conditions.

Responsibilities for Developers and Deployers: Developers must establish and document a thorough risk management framework, while deployers should monitor real-world usage and alert developers to any emerging issues. Both parties should collaborate to ensure the AI system remains safe and effective in clinical practice.

Post-Market Surveillance and Continuous Monitoring

Finally, let's address post-market surveillance and continuous monitoring, which the AI Act mandates for high-risk AI applications in real-world use.

Post-Market Surveillance Requirements: Once an AI system is deployed, developers and deployers must monitor its performance and promptly address any issues.

The AI Act outlines specific surveillance actions:

Performance Tracking: Regularly review how the AI system functions in real clinical settings. For instance, if a diagnostic tool frequently produces false positives or fails to identify certain conditions, these incidents should be documented and reported.

Incident Reporting and Corrective Actions: If an adverse event occurs — such as a misdiagnosis attributed to an AI system — it must be reported to regulatory authorities. Developers should work with deployers to implement corrective measures, update the system if necessary, and prevent recurrence.

Continuous Improvement Based on Real-World Data: The data collected through post-market surveillance is valuable for continuous improvement.

Regular System Updates: Based on performance data, AI models may require updates or retraining to maintain accuracy and relevance, particularly as clinical practices or patient populations evolve.

Adaptive Risk Management: Continuous monitoring allows

developers to adapt risk management measures as new challenges emerge in clinical environments.

Responsibilities for Developers and Deployers: Developers are responsible for providing tools and support for post-market monitoring, while deployers in clinical settings must ensure compliance with monitoring protocols, reporting any incidents and collaborating on system improvements.

Conclusion and Key Compliance Takeaways

To summarize, complying with the AI Act in biomedical engineering requires a proactive, collaborative approach to documentation, risk management, and post-market monitoring.

Here are three key takeaways to guide your work:

Comprehensive Documentation is essential for meeting regulatory standards and providing transparency to end-users.

Ongoing Risk Management ensures that your AI system remains safe and effective, adapting to new challenges as they arise.

Post-Market Surveillance is crucial for continuous improvement and regulatory alignment, enabling real-world data to inform the evolution of your AI systems.

By prioritizing these compliance requirements, you're not only meeting legal obligations but also building a foundation of trust and safety, ultimately advancing responsible innovation in healthcare.

Next, we'll move into a step-by-step compliance process for AI-driven medical devices, giving you practical tools to implement these requirements effectively.

Compliance Workflow For AI Projects in Biomedicine

Step-by-step walkthrough with visual aids and real-world examples. Overview of a typical compliance workflow, including: Initial risk assessment procedures. Required documentation and technical specifications. Interaction with regulatory bodies and use of "notified bodies" for third-party assessment. Breakdown of compliance steps to be considered at each phase of project development.

This segment will walk through the step-by-step process to ensure compliance with the AI Act from the early stages of development through post-market deployment. This practical guide will cover initial risk assessments, required documentation, interaction with regulatory bodies, and the role of "notified bodies" in third-party assessment. Let's dive into how each phase aligns with regulatory requirements, supported by visual aids and real-world examples.

Initial Risk Assessment Procedures

The compliance journey for any AI-driven biomedical project begins with an initial risk assessment, which lays the foundation for safe and ethical development.

Identify the Level of Risk: Under the AI Act, all AI applications must be assessed to determine their risk category. AI systems used in medical diagnostics or patient monitoring are generally classified as high-risk, given their potential impact on health and safety.

Define Potential Risks: Document and analyze potential risks that could impact patient safety or clinical outcomes. For example, in an AI-driven diagnostic tool, risks may include false positives/negatives, data biases, or failure to detect specific conditions.

Develop Mitigation Strategies: Once risks are identified, outline specific strategies to mitigate these risks. For instance, using diverse and representative datasets can help address bias in the model's training phase, while setting up alerts for unusual outputs can help detect errors early in deployment.

Visual Aid: A flowchart showing the risk assessment process, highlighting each step and examples of common risks in medical AI applications.

Required Documentation and Technical Specifications

Documentation is the backbone of compliance for high-risk AI systems, and it's essential to maintain comprehensive records at each stage of development. The AI Act requires extensive technical documentation to demonstrate regulatory compliance and ensure transparency.

Data Documentation: For biomedical AI systems, start by detailing data sources, collection methods, and quality control processes. Include information on how the data was cleaned, anonymized, and preprocessed to protect patient privacy and ensure compliance with both the AI Act and GDPR.

Model Specifications and Functional Descriptions: Provide a detailed description of the AI model's architecture, functions, and decision-making processes. This should include:

Explanation of the Model's Purpose: A clear description of the model's intended function, such as detecting cardiovascular conditions in early stages.

Description of Algorithms and Parameters: Details on the algorithms, feature selection, and model parameters used in development.

Accuracy, Reliability, and Limitations: Evidence from testing and validation phases showing how well the model performs, along with an outline of its limitations and conditions where it may be less effective.

Risk Management Documentation: Include all identified risks, mitigation measures, and records of ongoing risk assessments. Each update or modification to the model should trigger a new risk review and be documented accordingly.

Real-World Example: In a recent development of an AI-based diagnostic tool for lung cancer, developers meticulously documented the source and quality of imaging data, the model's accuracy in detecting nodules, and the specific conditions under which the AI tool might be less effective, such as low-resolution imaging.

Visual Aid: A checklist summarizing essential documentation components, from data sources and model specifications to ongoing risk management records.

Interaction with Regulatory Bodies and Notified Bodies

A critical part of the compliance workflow involves engagement with regulatory bodies and notified bodies for certification. For high-risk medical AI systems, an independent conformity assessment by a notified body is often required to verify compliance before the product enters the market.

Initial Consultations with Regulatory Authorities: Early in the development process, developers should consult with relevant regulatory bodies to ensure that their AI system meets current standards. In the EU, the European Medicines Agency (EMA) or similar national authorities may provide guidance specific to AI in healthcare.

Working with Notified Bodies for Conformity Assessment: Notified bodies are authorized third-party organizations that conduct impartial assessments of high-risk AI systems. Their role includes:

Evaluating the AI System's Compliance: The notified body reviews the AI system's documentation, risk management records, and technical specifications to verify compliance with the AI Act's safety and transparency requirements.

Conducting Testing and Issuing Certifications: If the AI system passes the evaluation, the notified body issues a conformity certification, allowing the system to be marketed within the EU.

Preparing for the Assessment: Prior to engaging a notified body, ensure that all documentation is complete and accessible. This includes technical specifications, risk assessments, and details on post-market surveillance plans. Clear, well-organized documentation can streamline the assessment process, reducing delays and feedback cycles.

Visual Aid: Diagram of the interaction flow between developers, regulatory bodies, and notified bodies, highlighting the certification process and requirements for market entry.

Breakdown of Compliance Steps at Each Phase of Development

A compliant AI workflow involves distinct compliance steps at each phase, from design through deployment and ongoing monitoring. Here's a phase-by-phase breakdown:

Design Phase

Set Compliance Goals: Begin by defining compliance goals based on the AI Act's requirements, focusing on risk management, transparency, and data quality.

Integrate Ethical Design Principles: Incorporate principles of transparency, fairness, and accountability into the design process, aligning with the ethical standards of healthcare.

Initial Documentation Setup: Create templates for risk management, technical documentation, and transparency reporting to be updated throughout the project.

Development and Testing Phase

Conduct Iterative Risk Assessments: Regularly assess and update risk mitigation measures as the AI model evolves. Document each iteration of the model, particularly when new data sources or algorithms are introduced.

Run Extensive Validation Tests: Validate the AI model on a broad range of scenarios to ensure its reliability, accuracy, and safety across diverse patient groups.

Compile Technical Documentation: Keep records of all model changes, data updates, and testing outcomes, ensuring that each update adheres to the AI Act's documentation standards.

Deployment Phase

Implement Transparency Measures: Ensure that users, such as healthcare providers, have access to detailed but understandable documentation on the AI system's functions, accuracy, and limitations.

Engage Notified Bodies for Certification: Submit all required documentation and evidence of compliance for conformity assessment, collaborating with the notified body as needed for certification.

Prepare Training Materials for End-Users: Develop clear training materials for healthcare providers to understand the AI system's outputs, supporting its responsible and effective use in clinical settings.

Post-Market Monitoring Phase

Establish Surveillance Protocols: Set up a continuous monitoring system to track the AI system's performance, collecting data on incidents, feedback, and clinical outcomes.

Regularly Update the Model: Adjust or retrain the AI model based on real-world data and emerging healthcare needs. Each update should trigger a new risk assessment and be documented accordingly.

Report Incidents to Regulatory Authorities: If adverse events occur, report them to the relevant authorities, and collaborate with notified bodies to implement corrective measures.

Visual Aid: Timeline infographic showing each compliance step across the phases of development, testing, deployment, and post-market monitoring.

Conclusion and Key Points

To summarize, a compliance workflow for AI-driven biomedical projects involves structured steps from risk assessment and documentation through regulatory engagement and post-market surveillance.

Here are the key points to remember:

Risk Assessment and Documentation are Continuous: Start early and maintain thorough documentation at every stage to simplify regulatory interactions and certification.

Collaboration with Notified Bodies: Engage notified bodies proactively for high-risk systems to secure necessary certifications for market entry.

Ongoing Monitoring and Adaptation: Compliance is a continuous process that extends beyond deployment, requiring regular performance monitoring and adaptive changes to meet evolving clinical needs.

By following this workflow, you ensure that your AI systems not only comply with regulatory requirements but also meet the ethical and safety standards critical in healthcare innovation.

Next, we'll move into a case study application, where you'll put this workflow into practice with a hypothetical AI project in biomedical engineering.

Case Study: Ensuring Compliance in AI-Driven Biomedical Devices

Practical case study with guided group discussion. Participants work in groups to apply compliance steps to a hypothetical biomedical AI device. Each group identifies key compliance actions, evaluates risks, and proposes monitoring and documentation strategies. Facilitated discussion to review solutions, emphasizing best practices and potential compliance pitfalls.

In this session, we'll take a practical approach to applying the compliance steps discussed. Working in groups, you'll assess a hypothetical biomedical AI device, identify key compliance actions, evaluate risks, and propose strategies for monitoring and documentation.

This exercise will allow you to apply the compliance workflow in real-time, examining potential challenges and solutions. After group discussions, we'll review each group's findings and highlight best practices, common pitfalls, and strategies for successful compliance.

Case Study Scenario: AI-Powered Heart Monitoring Device Background Imagine you're part of a team developing an AI-powered wearable heart monitoring device designed to detect early warning signs of arrhythmias and other cardiovascular conditions. This device continuously monitors vital signs, sending alerts to both patients and healthcare providers when it detects abnormalities. Because of its direct impact on patient health, this AI device is classified as high-risk under the AI Act and must meet the Act's stringent requirements for safety, transparency, risk management, and continuous monitoring. In this scenario, your task is to ensure compliance from initial development through post-market monitoring.

Group Work Instructions

Each group will focus on specific areas of compliance for this hypothetical device. We'll address the following points in each group:

Identify Key Compliance Actions: Determine which compliance steps are necessary to ensure regulatory alignment.

Evaluate Potential Risks and Mitigation Strategies: Identify and assess risks associated with the device and propose strategies for managing them.

Propose Monitoring and Documentation Strategies: Outline approaches for post-market surveillance and documentation that would satisfy the AI Act's requirements.

Group Assignments

Each group will work on one of the following key areas of compliance. Afterward, we'll reconvene for a facilitated discussion to review your findings.

Group 1: Compliance Actions and Documentation Task:

Determine the key compliance actions and documentation needed for the AI heart monitoring device.

Consider the following points.

Documentation Requirements: What specific technical documentation would you create for this device? Think about what regulators will need to understand its functionality, reliability, and safety.

Transparency with Users: How will you ensure that both patients and healthcare providers understand how the device works, including its limitations and intended uses?

Conformity Assessment with Notified Bodies: What steps would you take to prepare for and undergo a conformity assessment with a notified body?

Consider what information the notified body will need for certification.

Expected Outcome: Your group should outline a comprehensive list of documentation and describe how it would be organized to support both regulatory compliance and user transparency.

Group 2: Risk Evaluation and Mitigation Strategies Task:

Conduct a risk evaluation and propose mitigation strategies for the device.

Consider the following points.

Identifying Potential Risks: What are the primary risks associated with using this AI device, both in terms of patient safety and device reliability? For instance, think about risks related to false alarms, data biases, device malfunctions, and user misunderstandings.

Risk Mitigation: What specific measures would you implement to mitigate these risks? For example, could you use diverse data sources to prevent bias, or implement multiple safety checks to confirm arrhythmia detections?

Ongoing Risk Management: How would you ensure that risk assessments continue after deployment? Describe any procedures you would establish for regular re-evaluation.

Expected Outcome: Your group should produce a risk assessment overview that includes identified risks, proposed mitigation strategies, and a plan for ongoing risk management.

Group 3: Post-Market Monitoring and Continuous Compliance Task:

Design a monitoring and documentation strategy to ensure continuous compliance after the device is deployed.

Consider the following points.

Post-Market Surveillance Plan: How would you monitor the device's real-world performance? Think about collecting user feedback, tracking alerts, and recording any adverse incidents or errors.

Incident Reporting: What protocol would you establish for reporting incidents to regulatory bodies? Describe the type of incidents that would trigger reporting and the timeline for notification.

Continuous Improvement and Updates: How would you manage updates to the AI model to address any emerging issues or performance limitations? Consider how you would document changes and re-evaluate risks for each update.

Expected Outcome: Your group should create an outline of the post-market monitoring plan, including incident reporting steps and strategies for continuous improvement.

Group Discussion

Once each group has completed their discussion and documented their findings, we'll reconvene for a review and facilitated discussion. Each group will have a few minutes to present their key compliance actions, risk assessments, and monitoring strategies.

Group Presentations:

Group 1 (Compliance Actions and Documentation): Share your list of essential compliance actions and documentation strategies. What approach did you take to ensure transparency for end-users? How would you prepare for a notified body assessment?

Group 2 (Risk Evaluation and Mitigation): Present your risk assessment overview, describing the primary risks identified and your mitigation strategies. What considerations were most critical in developing your risk management plan?

Group 3 (Post-Market Monitoring and Continuous Compliance): Explain your post-market monitoring plan, detailing how you would track real-world performance and report incidents. What steps would you take to maintain continuous compliance?

Key Points and Takeaways from the Discussion

After all groups have presented, we'll highlight the key points from each compliance area, along with best practices and potential compliance pitfalls to be aware of.

Thorough Documentation and Transparent Communication: Comprehensive documentation and user-friendly communication materials are essential, not only for regulatory compliance but also for building user trust and understanding.

Proactive Risk Management: Effective risk management starts with identifying potential issues early and continues with regular re-evaluation after deployment. Key strategies include diverse data use to prevent biases, clear communication of limitations, and ongoing safety checks.

Robust Post-Market Surveillance: Continuous monitoring and timely incident reporting help maintain compliance and support improvements based on real-world data. Adaptability is crucial, especially as new challenges or needs arise in clinical settings.

This case study highlights how a structured compliance

workflow helps ensure that AI-driven biomedical devices meet the highest standards of safety, transparency, and reliability. By embedding compliance in each phase, from design to post-market monitoring, you create a foundation for responsible innovation that supports both patient welfare and regulatory alignment.

This concludes the interactive case study. Next, we'll summarize key takeaways and provide additional resources to support your ongoing compliance efforts.

Practical Tools And Resources For Compliance

Resource sharing and tool demonstration. Introduction to digital tools, templates, and resources available for managing compliance, including documentation templates, risk assessment tools, and checklists. Tips on organizing compliance documentation to meet the AI Act's transparency and accountability requirements.

Documentation templates are fundamental for keeping records consistent, clear, and easy to update. These templates support the transparency and accountability requirements of the AI Act, ensuring that you have comprehensive documentation ready for internal reviews or external assessments.

Technical Documentation Template: This template should cover the AI model's purpose, functionality, data sources, and any processing steps. Designed to meet regulatory standards, it also includes sections on system architecture, training methodologies, and key performance indicators.

Risk Management Template: This document helps structure your risk assessments, capturing identified risks, mitigation strategies, and regular re-evaluation points. Using a standardized template for risk management keeps your records organized and provides clear, accessible information on safety measures and model limitations.

User Guide Template: Intended for clinicians and healthcare providers, this template outlines the AI system's intended use, operational guidelines, and known limitations. It's written in accessible language to ensure that end-users can interpret and rely on the AI system effectively.

These templates are part of a digital compliance repository where team members can easily access and update documents as needed. This structure supports both internal alignment and streamlined external assessments.

Risk Assessment and Management Tools

Effective risk assessment is a dynamic, ongoing process, and digital tools can simplify this task by enabling comprehensive, real-time evaluations.

Digital Risk Assessment Platforms: Tools like LogicManager or RiskWatch offer automated risk assessment and reporting features. These platforms help you monitor potential risks at every development stage, assess risk levels, and document mitigation actions.

Bias Detection and Mitigation Tools: Tools such as Aequitas or Fairlearn help detect and address biases in AI models. These are particularly useful in biomedical AI, where ensuring that training data is representative and free from bias is critical to safe, equitable performance.

Version Control for Compliance: Using a platform like GitHub or GitLab for version control ensures that any model adjustments are carefully tracked and documented. This is especially helpful in post-market settings, where updates and modifications need to be documented with clear records of changes.

Set up periodic reminders within these tools to prompt regular risk assessments and data evaluations. This habit can help you maintain a proactive approach to compliance, keeping risks up-to-date and visible throughout the project.

Post-Market Monitoring and Incident Reporting

Tools For high-risk AI systems, the AI Act mandates post-market monitoring, making it essential to use tools that support continuous compliance and real-world performance tracking.

Surveillance and Monitoring Tools: Platforms like Qualio or Greenlight Guru are designed specifically for post-market monitoring in healthcare. These tools allow you to track system performance, gather user feedback, and record any incidents or adverse events, ensuring that real-world data informs continuous compliance.

Incident Reporting Templates and Automation: Automated incident reporting systems can help streamline the process of documenting and reporting issues to regulatory authorities. For example, Zendesk or JIRA can be adapted for incident logging and reporting, providing an organized record of events, notifications, and resolution timelines.

Continuous Feedback Loops: Consider using survey and feedback tools like SurveyMonkey or Typeform for gathering ongoing input from healthcare providers and patients. Regular feedback helps identify emerging issues or limitations, which can then be addressed proactively.

Create a compliance dashboard within these tools that highlights incident reports, user feedback, and system updates. This dashboard provides an at-a-glance view of compliance status, helping you spot patterns and respond quickly.

Checklists for Compliance Milestones

Compliance checklists are invaluable for keeping your project on track and ensuring that you don't miss any regulatory steps. These checklists are designed to guide you through each phase of compliance, from development to deployment and beyond.

Pre-Development Checklist: This checklist covers all preparatory compliance steps, including initial risk assessment, data privacy considerations, and setting up documentation systems. Starting with a solid foundation helps avoid compliance setbacks later on.

Deployment Checklist: Focused on final compliance checks before market release, this checklist includes notified body engagement, final documentation reviews, and user training preparation.

Post-Market Monitoring Checklist: This checklist ensures that you're meeting ongoing monitoring obligations, covering incident reporting, system updates, and regular risk reassessments.

Review and update checklists at each project milestone to ensure they reflect the latest compliance requirements. These can be embedded in your project management tools like Asana or Trello for easy tracking.

Organizing and Maintaining a Compliance Repository

A centralized compliance repository is essential for organizing documentation and tracking regulatory milestones. This repository serves as a digital archive for all compliance-related documents, templates, and records.

Compliance Repository Structure: Divide the repository into sections for each project phase, such as "Development," "Deployment," and "Post-Market Monitoring." Within each section, include folders for technical documentation, risk assessments, incident reports, and version-controlled updates.

Access Control and Updates: Ensure that access to the compliance repository is controlled, with editing permissions granted to relevant team members. Regularly review and update files to keep all compliance documents current.

Audit Readiness: Maintaining a well-organized repository simplifies audit preparation, as all required documents are stored in one place and easily accessible for regulatory review.

Use a platform like SharePoint, Confluence, or a cloud storage solution with strong version control to keep the repository organized and secure.

The tools and resources introduced today provide a robust framework for managing AI Act compliance in biomedical projects.

Here are a few key points to keep in mind:

Documentation and Templates help structure your compliance efforts, ensuring that critical information is recorded and accessible.

Risk Assessment Tools support ongoing risk management, enabling a proactive approach to compliance.

Monitoring and Incident Reporting Platforms facilitate continuous compliance, ensuring real-world data informs improvements and maintains regulatory alignment.

With these tools, you're well-equipped to integrate compliance into every stage of your AI projects, supporting both innovation and regulatory accountability in biomedical engineering.

Interactive Q&A and Compliance Challenges

Open floor for participant questions. Discussion of specific compliance challenges in AI for biomedicine, allowing participants to seek guidance on their own project concerns. Focus on proactive risk management and strategies for ongoing compliance beyond the initial stages of development.

To help focus our conversation, let's consider a few key areas where compliance challenges often arise. Feel free to raise questions on these topics or any other concerns you might have:

Proactive Risk Management in Dynamic Environments

How can teams manage emerging risks effectively in AI systems that evolve post-deployment?

For high-risk biomedical AI, proactive risk management is crucial, especially as real-world data can reveal new issues that were not apparent in initial testing. Consider asking about best practices for setting up adaptable risk protocols that adjust as your AI system encounters varied clinical scenarios.

Strategies for Continuous Compliance

What practical steps can be taken to ensure ongoing compliance beyond the initial development stage?

Continuous monitoring, regular system updates, and re-assessment of risk are required by the AI Act. This can become challenging as new data inputs, updates, or regulatory changes arise. Let's discuss ways to build compliance into project workflows, so teams can stay aligned with evolving standards and performance expectations.

Real-World Challenges with Transparency and User Communication

Maintaining transparency with end-users - particularly clinicians and patients - can present unique challenges, especially when balancing complex AI explanations with accessibility.

How do we keep users informed about the AI system's functionality, limitations, and updates without overwhelming them?

This is especially relevant in healthcare, where clear communication can impact the trust and effectiveness of AI applications.

Key Discussion Points

During this Q&A, we'll focus on addressing practical challenges and potential solutions, including:

Flexible Compliance Frameworks: How to set up compliance frameworks that can adapt as your AI project progresses. This might involve discussing the role of version control for documentation, streamlined reporting systems, or effective ways to track real-world performance data.

Incident Response and Reporting: Guidance on setting up effective incident reporting and response protocols.

What types of incidents require immediate reporting, and how can teams prepare for them?

We'll also cover strategies for analyzing incident data to improve future iterations.

Resource Allocation for Long-term Compliance: Compliance isn't just a one-time task, so let's explore strategies for allocating resources to support ongoing compliance. This may include tips on leveraging existing tools or setting up dedicated teams to monitor and update compliance-related aspects of your AI system.

As we wrap up the Q&A, here are a few final takeaways:

Embed Compliance in Everyday Operations: Compliance should become an integral part of the workflow, embedded in every phase of your AI project from development through post-market use. Building it into daily operations, rather than treating it as an add-on, ensures smoother alignment with the AI Act.

Adopt a Culture of Continuous Improvement: By treating compliance as an ongoing process rather than a one-time task, teams can stay ahead of regulatory requirements and proactively address emerging risks.

Maintaining compliance in AI-driven biomedicine is challenging but manageable with the right strategies in place. This discussion highlighted ways to embed compliance within your projects effectively, supporting both innovation and regulatory alignment.

Recap And Key Compliance Takeaways

Summary of core points, emphasizing the need for thorough documentation, proactive risk management, and effective use of monitoring tools.

As we conclude today's seminar, let's recap the core points we've covered and focus on the essential practices for compliance with the AI Act in biomedical projects. These practices not only help meet regulatory standards but also enhance the safety, transparency, and reliability of AI-driven healthcare solutions.

Thorough Documentation is the backbone of compliance.

Each phase of your AI project requires clear, detailed records — from initial data sourcing and model development through to deployment and post-market activities.

This documentation must include:

Technical Specifications: A detailed outline of the AI model's functionality, data sources, and performance metrics.

Risk Management Records: A log of identified risks, mitigation strategies, and ongoing assessments.

User Documentation: Information that's accessible to clinicians and end-users, highlighting the system's limitations and intended uses. Proper documentation not only supports regulatory assessments but also promotes transparency and trust with end-users.

Proactive, iterative risk management is critical, especially for high-risk AI systems in healthcare.

Effective risk management includes:

Early and Ongoing Assessments: Identify potential risks at the outset and re-evaluate them with each major update or real-world use case.

Bias Mitigation: Use diverse, high-quality datasets and regularly assess the model for biases to ensure fair outcomes across patient demographics.

Adaptability: Set up flexible risk management protocols that can adjust based on new data or evolving clinical needs. A proactive approach helps prevent issues before they escalate, safeguarding patient outcomes and ensuring regulatory alignment.

Continuous monitoring is essential for ensuring that the AI system performs as intended once deployed.

Monitoring and incident reporting should include:

Real-World Performance Tracking: Collect and analyze real-world data to identify any discrepancies in system performance and address them promptly.

Incident Response Plans: Establish clear protocols for documenting and reporting incidents to regulatory authorities. Ensure that your team understands what constitutes an incident and how to respond quickly.

Feedback Loops: Regularly gather feedback from end-users, such as healthcare providers and patients, to inform updates and adjustments. Monitoring supports both compliance and continuous improvement, helping to adapt the AI system as new challenges arise.

By embedding thorough documentation, proactive risk management, and continuous monitoring into your workflow, you're well-equipped to navigate the AI Act's requirements and deliver safe, trustworthy AI solutions in healthcare. We look forward to seeing how you apply these principles in your work.

Closing Remarks

As we conclude this Seminar, I'd like to emphasize that aligning AI innovations with regulatory standards is both a responsibility and an opportunity.

By following the principles we've discussed, you're not only ensuring compliance but also contributing to a future where AI enhances healthcare in safe, ethical, and impactful ways.

We look forward to seeing how you apply these insights in your work and continue advancing AI responsibly within biomedical engineering. Please feel free to reach out with any questions or for additional guidance, by email to: roberto.sammarchi@unibo.it

Workshop Forms

Form 1: Identifying Key Compliance Challenges

This form focuses on identifying and addressing compliance challenges in the development of a high-risk AI diagnostic tool, classified under the AI Act.

1. Data Quality and Diversity issues:

What challenges might arise in ensuring the training data is representative and free from biases?

How would you address any data quality issues impacting accuracy or fairness?

2. Risk Management issues:

What potential risks could this diagnostic tool pose (e.g., false positives/negatives, data privacy concerns)?

How will you assess and mitigate these risks during development and post-market phases?

3. Documentation issues:

What technical documentation should be prepared to comply with the AI Act?

How will you fulfill transparency requirements for regulatory purposes?

Form 2: Developing a Risk Management and Monitoring Strategy

This form is designed to create a risk management and monitoring strategy aligned with the AI Act's requirements for high-risk devices.

1. Risk Assessment Protocols issues:

Outline a risk assessment protocol for all development phases.

How will you address issues like biases, model accuracy, and clinical errors?

2. Post-Market Surveillance issues:

Develop a plan for post-market monitoring to ensure the tool performs effectively in clinical settings.

What mechanisms will you use to gather real-world performance data and respond to emerging risks?

3. Incident Reporting issues:

How will you comply with incident reporting requirements?

If unexpected results arise, how will you document, report, and address these issues?

Form 3: Planning for Transparency and User Communication

This form emphasizes ensuring transparency for both clinicians and patients using the diagnostic tool.

1. User Documentation issues:

What information should be included in the user documentation for healthcare providers?

How can you ensure that clinicians understand the tool's functionality, limitations, andaccuracy?

2. Patient Transparency issues:

How will you communicate to patients that an AI system is involved in their diagnosis?

How can you address patient concerns about privacy, reliability, and accuracy in non-technical terms?

3. Regular Updates issues:

How will you provide users with updates on changes, improvements, or emerging

limitations of the tool?

What strategies will ensure transparency throughout the tool's lifecycle?

Key Checklists

Risk Assessment Checklist

Use this checklist to comprehensively evaluate risks associated with AI projects in biomedical applications.

☐ Is the dataset representative of diverse populations and free from biases?

☐ Have potential biases in the data or model been identified, documented, and addressed?

☐ Is the model validated for accuracy and fairness across all relevant demographics?

☐ Are safety measures implemented and tested during all phases of development and deployment?

☐ Have mechanisms for ongoing post-market surveillance been set up to monitor performance and safety?

☐ Are risk management processes documented and updated regularly based on new data?

☐ Has an independent review of safety standards been conducted?

☐ Are there contingency plans for addressing unexpected risks or system failures?

Compliance-by-Design Checklist

Ensure compliance with the AI Act by following these steps throughout the AI development lifecycle.

☐ Are AI Act regulations reviewed and incorporated during the initial design phase?

☐ Are risk management protocols systematically embedded at each development stage?

☐ Are documentation practices comprehensive and aligned with AI Act requirements?

☐ Is post-market monitoring included in the operational plan with clearly defined protocols?

☐ Have ethical considerations, such as patient privacy and consent, been thoroughly addressed?

☐ Are compliance audits scheduled at regular intervals to ensure ongoing alignment?

☐ Have user-facing materials been designed to comply with transparency requirements?

☐ Are all team members trained on compliance-by-design principles and regulatory standards?

Best Pracces Checklist

Adopt these best practices to ensure that AI integration in biomedical engineering is aligned with safety, transparency, and ethical standards.

☐ Are transparency strategies for clinicians and patients clearly defined and implemented?

☐ Is the data governance framework robust, well-documented, and aligned with ethical standards?

☐ Have the impacts of the AI system on patient trust and clinical workflows been evaluated?

☐ Are continuous monitoring and regular model updates planned and documented for post-deployment?

☐ Have the limitations, capabilities, and intended uses of the AI system been clearly documented?

☐ Is there a process to collect and respond to feedback from end users and stakeholders?

☐ Have the data sources been verified for quality,

representativeness, and compliance with GDPR?

☐ Are training datasets regularly updated to reflect the latest developments and demographics?

☐ Are educational resources provided to end users to support informed and ethical use of the AI system?

About The Author

Roberto Sammarchi

Lawyer qualified to practice before higher courts, recognized by the Italian National Bar Council as a specialist in information law, digital communication, and data protection. After studying computational linguistics applied to legal texts and earning a PhD in the design and analysis of legal information systems, he has spent nearly forty years guiding companies and organizations in innovation and digital transformation projects, with a focus on legal compliance. A certified innovation manager registered with the Italian Ministry of Enterprises and Made in Italy, he has also taught in the master's program in Clinical Engineering and Medical Devices at the University of Bologna since 2007.

www.ingramcontent.com/pod-product-compliance
Lightning Source LLC
Chambersburg PA
CBHW070414230526
45471CB00006B/2800